Discard

Calling Car 24 Frank
A DAY WITH THE POLICE

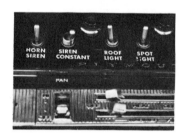

Calling Car 24 Frank
A DAY WITH THE POLICE

Written and Photographed
by Rona Beame

JULIAN MESSNER NEW YORK

Published by Julian Messner, a Division of Simon & Schuster, Inc.
1 West 39 Street, New York, N.Y. 10018. All rights reserved.

Printed in the United States of America
ISBN 0-671-32506-X Cloth Trade
ISBN 0-671-32507-8 MCE

Library of Congress Catalog Card No. 70-180530
Design by Marjorie Zaum K.

Third Printing, 1975

For Buddy, Andrew, and Richard

Roy
Pannenbacker

Rashid
Abdul-Rahim

This book is about two policemen—Roy Pannenbacker and Rashid Abdul-Rahim. They are partners and ride in a patrol car in the 24th Precinct, one of the most crowded and busy areas in New York City. All kinds of people live there—whites, blacks, Puerto Ricans, Dominicans; some of the richest and most famous people in the city, and some of the poorest.

The policemen in the 24th never know what their next call will be. It could be a murder or a family argument; a boy crying over a stolen bicycle or an actress reporting a robbery of thousands of dollars. Or the next call could be a phony, and suddenly someone who doesn't like the police is shooting at them. It doesn't happen often. But they never know when it could.

All the policemen in the 24th work hard. But Roy and Rashid like it that way. They like meeting and helping all kinds of people. They like the excitement of knowing that when they get up in the morning, anything can happen that day.

7

4:30 A.M.

Roy's alarm clock rings.

"At 4:30 in the morning, it looks like the middle of the night, and it sure feels like it. All I want to do," Roy says, "is stay in that bed and go back to sleep. But once I get the razor on my face and hit the shower—a very hot one—I'm awake."

Roy has a quick breakfast, and by 5 A.M. he's out of the house. He drives from his home in Selden, Long Island, to Ronkonkoma, a nearby town, where he catches the 5:32 A.M. train to the city. The train trip lasts almost an hour and a half, and Roy often uses the time to catch up on his sleep.

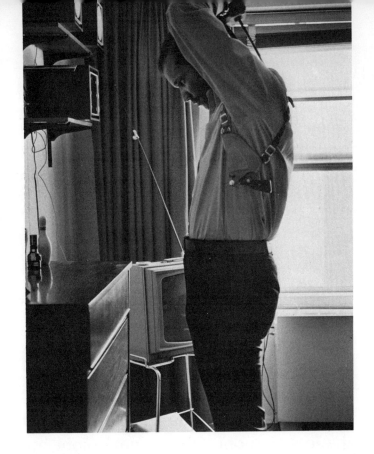

6:00 A.M.

While Roy is riding into the city, Rashid is waking up.

"I never use an alarm clock. I just somehow wake up. But it's one thing to wake up, and another to get out of bed. It takes me at least fifteen minutes to crawl out. I get into a cold shower—and then I'm up."

Rashid dresses quickly and slips on his gun, which he must carry with him at all times, even when he is off-duty. He drinks some orange juice and takes a vitamin pill, and by 6:35 A.M. he is out of the house. He drives from the Bronx, where he lives, into Manhattan.

7:20 A.M.

Roy and Rashid arrive at the station house. This week they are working the 8 A.M. to 4 P.M. shift. There are three shifts each day: 8 A.M. to 4 P.M., 4 P.M. to midnight, and midnight to 8 A.M. Roy and Rashid work a different shift each week.

They change into their uniforms downstairs in the locker room. For the next eight hours, they will ride together in a radio patrol car.

"It's like having a second wife," Roy says. "In fact, you spend more time with your car partner than you do with your wife. So you've got to get along."

"If you don't," Rashid adds, "it's a disaster. Just try spending eight hours a day in a car with someone you don't like."

7:50 A.M.

Roll call. The sergeant reads off the names of the men on the shift. (There are seventy-five men working this shift.) He explains any special instructions for the day.

Then the shift begins. The men in the 24th Precinct cover the Upper West Side of Manhattan, from 86th Street to 110th Street.

There are seventy-seven precincts in New York City. Each day at this time, about 7,600 policemen turn out to patrol the streets of the city.

8:00 A.M.

Roy and Rashid start out in their patrol car. Each car (and foot patrolman) is assigned a sector or area to patrol. Roy and Rashid's sector goes from 107th Street to 110th Street, from Broadway to Central Park West. It is one of the busiest areas in the 24th Precinct.

"You never know what's going to happen next

13

in our sector," Roy says. "One minute you're dealing with a wino or junkie, and the next minute you're going up to one of the fanciest apartments in the city to investigate a robbery. It keeps you on your toes."

Today, Rashid takes the first shift as driver. While he drives, Roy keeps a complete record of each call in his memo book: the time of the call, the names and addresses of the people involved, and what has happened. After four hours, they will switch; Roy will drive and Rashid will keep the record.

As they drive slowly through their sector, both men keep an eye out for any trouble. They stop to talk to a shopkeeper who has been robbed several times. The shopkeeper has two big dogs. One of them runs out to greet Roy.

"Since I've gotten the dogs," the shopkeeper tells the two policemen, "no one has bothered my store."

"It's no wonder," Rashid says, laughing. "I wouldn't tangle with them myself."

8:08 A.M.

The car radio suddenly speaks: "24 Frank." ("24" refers to the "24th Precinct" and "Frank" is the code name for Roy and Rashid's sector.)

Roy picks up the phone. "24 Frank," he says.

The operator at police headquarters ("Central") says: "A 10-54 . . . 110th Street . . . Columbus and Amsterdam." (10-54 is police shorthand for a sick person.)

Roy answers: "10-4, Central." ("We're taking care of it.") And off they go.

On the sidewalk, an elderly man is lying unconscious. "Let's get him onto the grass," Roy says.

16

"The pavement's too hot."

Roy and Rashid gently lift the man onto the grass. Rashid loosens his clothes while Roy writes in his memo book the time, location, and a brief description of the man and his condition.

An ambulance arrives, and the man is placed on a stretcher. At the same time that "24 Frank" received this call, Central also dispatched an ambulance from the nearest city hospital.

Roy and Rashid escort the ambulance back to the hospital to make sure it gets there as quickly as possible.

At the hospital, the doctor tells Roy and Rashid that the man might have died if they hadn't got to him in time.

17

"When you can help someone like that, it really makes you feel good," Rashid says.

8:29 A.M.

As Roy and Rashid drive down 110th Street, they find that traffic is all jammed up. Roy gets out to take a look. He finds that a taxi cab has stalled in the middle of the street.

"Come on," he says to Rashid, "let's give this guy a push."

Rashid laughs. "And I used to think that all a

policeman did was chase criminals."

8:34 A.M.

The car radio is getting busier, but none of the calls are for "24 Frank." Then one comes. It's a 10-65. There is a "dangerous condition" on a side street. It turns out to be a big hole in the gutter.

"That's a beaut," Rashid says, as he examines the hole. "If a big truck came down this street, you'd wind up with a real mess."

While Roy blocks the street to all traffic, Rashid covers the hole with a big board until it can be fixed.

Then he calls the precinct so that the hole can be reported to the Highways Department for repair.

8:43 A.M.

Roy and Rashid are driving through their sector. They hear a gunshot. It sounds very loud in the quiet of the morning.

In an instant, Rashid turns the car around and Roy puts on the flashing red light and siren which are used when speed is necessary. The car flies up the street.

Now a call comes in over the car radio: "24 Frank...10-10...a gunshot...vicinity 107th Street." Central has received a report of the gunshot Roy and Rashid heard.

"We are on it already, Central," Roy answers as the car speeds to the scene.

They arrive and find the street empty, except for three people. A man and two women are staggering up the street. Roy and Rashid run after them. Rashid grabs the man and searches him.

"I had no idea what was happening," Rashid explains later. "You have two seconds to decide

20

what to do. The first thing to find out is if the guy has a weapon."

The man turns out to be unarmed and unhurt. Meanwhile, Roy questions the women. One of them bursts into tears.

She tells Roy that the man's brother, who is a junkie, has shot at them and then fled in a car. Roy realizes that the two women and the man on the street are also drug addicts.

"It's pretty easy to spot them," Roy explains: "Droopy eyelids, slurred speech, and sometimes even swollen hands and fingers."

After the woman stops crying, all three of them refuse to talk. They do not want to press charges against the man's brother. They just want to get away.

Drug addicts are not interested in cooperating with the police. Many of them have been in trouble with the police at one time or another for drug abuse.

But Roy and Rashid have not seen these people taking drugs or found any in their possession. They cannot arrest them just for being drug addicts. So they let them go.

At that moment, a man and a woman carrying a baby rush up to Roy and Rashid.

"I saw the whole thing," the woman tells them breathlessly. "When the man who fired the shot drove away, I jumped into my car and followed him. But I lost him at 120th Street." She gives them the color, make and license number of the car.

Roy calls Central and repeats the information. Central will send out a description of the car over the police radio.

Meanwhile, the sergeant arrives. He listens to all calls on his car radio, and helps out on the important or dangerous ones. Now he also questions the witness.

Rashid notices a bullet hole in the windshield of the woman's car. He points it out to her. She is amazed.

"I guess I was so excited that I didn't even notice it. It must have happened when the man was shooting at his brother. I wasn't in the car then."

Rashid looks for the bullet in her car. If he can find it, the police laboratory can tell what kind of gun it was fired from.

But Rashid cannot find the bullet. He and Roy head back to the station house to make a full report on the shooting.

"That lady sure was gutsy," Rashid says. "She took quite a chance following that guy."

At the station house, the police clerk types up the information. Even though Roy and Rashid keep a complete record of each call in their memo books, the police clerk still has to make a separate report. This is done on all calls that need further investigation, like a robbery or a murder, or calls that involve another city or state agency.

Detectives will follow up this case. "It's unlikely the detectives will ever find the guy who fired the shot," Roy says. "The car was probably stolen, and I'll bet he's gotten rid of it by now. What a bunch! A man who'd shoot at his own brother! But that's what dope does to you."

"Listen, dope addicts will steal from their own mother for the stuff," Rashid says. "The only person they care about is their pusher."

9:30 A.M.

While they are in the station house, Roy and Rashid decide to take off a few minutes to practice on the pistol range downstairs. All policemen are given fifty rounds of free ammunition each month for practice.

"We're only required to practice three times a year. But it's a good idea to do it more often,"

Rashid says. "You become rusty if you don't use your gun much, and shooting well is the best way to stay alive when there's real trouble."

10:00 A.M.

As they are driving away from the station house, "24 Frank" receives another urgent call. Someone has reported seeing an armed prowler on the roof of a tenement.

Roy turns on the flashing roof light. This time they don't use the siren because they don't want to warn the prowler. At each intersection Rashid slows down to make sure no cars are coming through. "There's no point in having an accident now," he says.

They arrive in front of an old, run-down tenement. Both men jump out of the car and run into the building. Roy goes up the stairs hugging the wall, his gun drawn.

Rashid waits a few moments and then follows. In one hand he clutches his night stick, while his other hand stays about two inches from his gun. No one is on the staircase.

28

They search the roof and fire escapes. Roy takes one side and Rashid the other. They find no one.

"A lot of the time there's no one there. Either

the guy's already gone or maybe there was no one there in the first place. But you never take a chance," Roy says. "Every time you go on a 'prowler run' or a 'burglary in progress,' you act like your life is in danger. And it is."

On their way downstairs, Roy tells Rashid: "Boy, I really appreciate it when you don't come up the stairs right behind me. If someone's waiting for us, we'd just make twice as big a target. Some of the guys I've worked with don't understand that. Or maybe they get careless. I don't know."

"I learned all about being careful in Vietnam," Rashid says with a smile.

"Yeah, that's how you stay alive," Roy says. "You know, I'll never forget when these two guys from another precinct went out on a prowler call. As they walked into the building, they were shot at by two snipers from across the street.

"It was a phony call and the snipers were waiting for them. They just had a gripe against the police and wanted to get themselves some cops. One of the policemen died, and the other is still paralyzed."

When Roy and Rashid walk out of the building, they find the sergeant's car in front. "Figured you

30

were up top," the sergeant tells them. "We were covering the front and rear for you."

"Good story," Rashid says laughing. "You just don't like running up all those stairs." They talk for a few minutes, and then the two cars drive away.

"I know it sounds corny," Rashid says, "but one of the nicest things about this job is the fellowship among policemen. You can meet a policeman anywhere—even in another city—and you've got something in common. They always ask if they can give you a hand—no matter what kind of problem you have.

"And when there's a 10-13—when a brother officer is in trouble—every policeman in the area turns on his siren and breaks his neck getting there. It's really something to know that all these other guys are willing to lay their lives on the line for you."

10:20 A.M.

A call comes over the radio that someone is having a heart attack. The family has called police emergency number 911 for help. Central has dispatched an ambulance and 24 Frank to the scene.

Rashid turns on the siren and roof light. This time they don't have to worry about warning anyone —just get there quickly. The car speeds down Columbus Avenue.

Inside the apartment they find an old man lying on his bed gasping for breath. His worried family stands around helplessly.

"He's in bad shape," Roy says to Rashid.

Rashid and Roy try to make the man more comfortable. Then Roy telephones Central from another room to make sure the ambulance is coming as fast as possible.

When Roy returns, the man seems in less pain

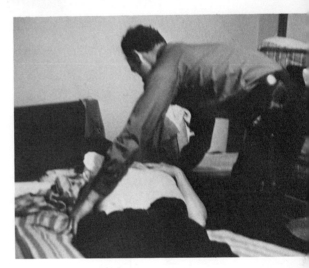

and looks as if he is going to sleep.

Roy acts quickly. He whacks the man on the chest. Then he bends down, puts his lips on the man's lips, and starts mouth-to-mouth resuscitation.

The man's family watches. No one in the room stirs. Finally, Roy stands up. "He's breathing again," he says with satisfaction.

The man had stopped breathing. Roy used the first-aid training that police receive. He smacked the man's chest to stimulate the heart muscle. With the mouth-to-mouth resuscitation, he helped the man start breathing again.

Rashid helps Roy prop the man up so he can breathe more easily. When the ambulance comes, the man is given oxygen and rushed to the hospital.

Back in the car, Rashid says, "When you were out of the room, I didn't realize the man was dying. He looked like he was going to sleep."

Roy smiles. "You've been on the Force for little over a year. I've been a policeman more than seven years. I've seen a lot of these cardiac cases."

"So much of the time," Rashid says, "a policeman has life and death in his hands. It's a heavy responsibility."

10:56 A.M.

Roy and Rashid get a 10-6. A large crowd has gathered on Broadway, and a storekeeper complained that they are blocking his entrance.

They find out that it is a rally organized by a local political club. Roy asks if they have a permit to conduct a rally. They don't.

Roy explains that they cannot have a rally on a public street without a permit. The crowd leaves.

Back in the car, Roy comments: "I did it as nicely as possible, so there would be no hard feelings. And they were pretty good about it. They just left quietly. Sometimes, it's not that easy. Some people get angry no matter what you do or how you do it. I've been called a pig—and worse things than that—just for telling people that they couldn't block up a street."

11:08 A.M.

"24 Frank . . . 10-23, bomb threat . . . P.S. 165 . . . 234 West . . . ." The street number is unclear.

"10-5 Street." Roy asks Central to repeat the street number.

"109th Street," Says Central loud and clear.

"10-4," says Roy.

When they arrive, they find the children in orderly groups moving away from the school. Inside

they speak to the principal, a teacher, and the sergeant. They learn that someone has called the school and warned that a bomb would go off.

Roy asks some questions:

What was the voice of the caller like? Was it an adult or a child? What were the exact words?

Who received the call?

Who is still left in the building, and where are they?

Where are the entrances to the building?

Where is the boiler room? (The boiler room is a good place to hide a bomb.)

Then he, Rashid, and two other policemen who have also answered the call divide up the building and start searching. They look behind radiators, under desks—anywhere that a bomb could be hidden.

Finally, they all meet downstairs. No one has found anything. "Nine out of ten times you won't find anything," Rashid says. "But it's that one time

you have to watch out for. So you always, always act as if there is a bomb. You never take a chance."

12:02 P.M.

Rashid drives away from the school. He glances at his watch and then pulls the car over to the curb. "It's 12. Your turn to drive," he tells Roy. They switch positions.

As Roy drives down the next block, they see a

car parked half on the sidewalk. "Will you look at that!" Rashid says. "I got a lot of sympathy for people trying to find parking spaces in the city, but that guy's gotta get a ticket."

12:07 P.M.

"24 Frank."

"Here we go again," Rashid says, lifting up the phone.

There has been a fight in an elementary school.

At the school, they learn that a boy pulled a knife in a fight with another boy. No one has been hurt, but the principal insists that the police arrest the boy with the knife. He is eleven years old.

40

Roy and Rashid take him back to the station house.

While they wait for the boy's father to come, Rashid questions the boy. "I tried to make him

understand that he is in real trouble—that he might be ruining his whole life. But he didn't take it seriously. He thinks it's all a big joke."

"We'll release the boy into his father's custody," Roy explains. "Now that he's been arrested, it's up to the courts. The judge will decide whether he's sent to a correctional school or not."

12:45 P.M.

Someone has turned in a lost pocketbook at the station house. It is given to Roy and Rashid to return.

Rashid finds the woman's address on a card

in the pocketbook. He climbs five flights of stairs to her apartment.

"She just couldn't believe it," Rashid tells Roy later. "Everything was there—her money, her charge cards, everything! It sure doesn't happen often. But when it does, you feel pretty good about people."

1:00 P.M.

Rashid looks at his watch. "Time for chow." He calls Central. "10-64," he tells them. ("The car will be out for an hour.")

They park and walk to a luncheonette on Broadway. While waiting for their food, they pull

out their memo books and start writing.

"When you get a lot of calls, you don't have the time to record everything on the spot," Rashid explains. "Lunch hour's a good time to catch up. Sometimes, we get fed up with all the writing, but we know it's important. If anyone ever needs to know anything about a case, we've got all the information here in our books. And if we have to be a witness in court a couple of months from now, we can look at our books and get all the facts."

2:00 P.M.

After lunch, they call Central and report that they are back at work again. A moment later they get a 10-30. There has been an armed robbery in a supermarket.

At the store, they learn that three men with guns held up the market when it was filled with customers. They stole several thousand dollars.

Roy and Rashid question the manager and the clerks. The store has been robbed before, and the manager is sure he recognized one of the holdup men.

44

Roy uses a police phone on the street to call the 24th Precinct. He describes the holdup men and gives other information on the robbery so that the detective unit can begin to follow up the case.

When Roy returns, Rashid says, "Those men have got to be dope addicts. No one else would be desperate enough to rob a crowded store. They would wait for a better time."

"Once a guy is hooked on dope," Roy says, "he'll do anything. If you're dumb enough to be killing yourself with drugs, robbing a crowded store isn't going to stop you.

"I always try to talk to the kids in this neighborhood about dope. 'See those junkies on the corner,' I'll say to them. 'You want to be like that? How old are you—fifteen? That guy on the corner is only eighteen. How old does he look? He looks like he's forty, right? And he's not going to live another five years if he keeps it up. You want that to happen to you?'"

2:20 P.M.

Driving up Amsterdam Avenue, they see a small crowd of people on the sidewalk. A woman steps out of the crowd and motions for them to stop. At the center of the crowd, a very small boy is sitting on the street, crying.

"He's lost," the woman tells them. "No one here knows who he is," says a shopkeeper.

"Don't worry, we'll take care of him," Rashid says. He lifts the boy and carries him over to the car. Rashid and Roy drive around the neighborhood and ask some of the shopkeepers if they recognize the boy. But no one does.

They return to the station house to find out if anyone has reported a missing child. While Rashid tries to comfort the boy, Roy calls Central and gives them a description. A few minutes later, Central calls back. They've just received a call that fits the description of the boy.

The boy lives in the 24th Precinct, so Roy and Rashid drive him home.

After the mother gives her child an enormous hug, she explains: "I was in a store shopping, and before I knew it, he was gone. I don't think I've ever been so scared in my life."

3:02 P.M.

As the afternoon wears on, its gets hotter. "We sure could use an air conditioner in this car," Roy says as he wipes his face with a handkerchief.

"Fat chance," says Rashid.

"You boil in the summer and freeze in the winter," Roy says. "But you're a lot better off in a car than on foot."

48

"When I was walking a beat last winter," Rashid says, "there were some days that were so cold I couldn't even feel my feet."

"Hey, we haven't gotten a call for five minutes," Roy remarks. "Today's a pretty busy day, but there are days you wouldn't believe. You don't have a minute between calls, and you're on the run all day long."

Just then the car radio blares: "24 Frank."

"You spoke too soon," Rashid says, picking up the phone. A fire hydrant opposite a school has been turned on.

Roy and Rashid arrive and find some children playing in the gushing water. "Sorry, but I've got to turn it off," Rashid tells them. The children don't object too much because they know that opening hydrants is against the law. Rashid explains to the children that if too many fire hydrants are turned on, there won't be enough water pressure for fighting fires. "If you go to the station house, they'll give you a sprinkler attachment for the hydrant," he tells them.

"When summer comes, living on some of these streets is no picnic," Rashid says later. "I think the

50

insides of those buildings are hotter than the streets. It's no wonder that by nighttime everybody sits outside on the steps."

3:19 P.M.

Roy and Rashid get another sick call. When they arrive, a large crowd has gathered around an eleven-year-old boy who is lying on a mat, covered with a blanket. He is crying, and his mother is trying

to comfort him.

Rashid speaks to the boy's mother. He finds out that the boy has fallen from a hotel awning and hurt his arm. The boy had been climbing after his ball, which was stuck on the awning.

Rashid tries to cheer up the boy. "When I broke my leg," Rashid tells him, "I bet it hurt worse than your arm does now." The boy smiles. "The ambulance will be here in a minute, and then you'll be fixed up in no time."

While Rashid talks to the boy, Roy tries to move the crowd back. "You've got to move people away from a person who's sick or hurt, so he can get air. You also have to make room for the stretcher to get through."

When the ambulance arrives, Roy helps lift the boy onto the stretcher. Afterwards, he turns to Rashid and says, "All that over a crummy fifteen-cent ball."

3:50 P.M.

No new calls are coming through. It's almost time to report back to the station house.

Roy and Rashid stop to talk to some of the neighborhood children. They know them from the days they direct traffic at school crossings.

Roy says later: "It's great when you've been in the same area for a while and the kids get to know you. After a while, when they see your car come by, they break their necks running down the stairs to give you a wave and shout, 'Hi, Officer Roy. How you doing?'

"I remember one afternoon, when we were going down Columbus Avenue and this guy comes running frantically out on the street. He can hardly speak English, but he motions us to come quickly.

"So we pull the car over and run in and here's this poor woman lying in bed. She's pregnant and ready to have the baby. So we deliver the baby.

"A couple of weeks later, riding past the same location again, there's the woman. She gives us a big wave and holds up the baby. She couldn't speak English, but just the expression on her face was enough."

4:00 P.M.

Roy and Rashid reach the station house. As they arrive, policemen from the next shift (4 P.M. to midnight) are leaving the station house to patrol their posts. Roy and Rashid sign out on the roll call sheet and change back into their civilian clothes.

"I don't have time to talk over the day with the

guys," Roy says. "I've got to catch the 4:41 train. If I don't, I get home much too late.

"If I'm tired, I sleep on the train. If not, I read or study. Right now I'm studying for the sergeant's exam. It's a tough exam. They give it every two years, and there are 25,000 guys competing for 600 positions. I'm also planning to go to college one day soon. When I retire from the police force, I want to teach. You can retire after twenty years and receive half-pay.

"When I first get home, I feel beat. But in warm weather like this, I take a swim and play with the kids, and pretty soon I feel fine. I've got two kids. Dawn is seven, and Roy, Jr., is three. And we're expecting a third pretty soon. I have a ball playing with my kids. I just wish I could spend more

time with them. That's probably the worst part of the job for me—working weekends, nights, and holidays. It's hard on my wife, Estelle, too."

Unlike Roy, Rashid doesn't go directly home after work. His wife, Eunice, works as a medical secretary in a hospital and doesn't get home until 5:30. So Rashid generally stops off at his parents' apartment first.

Rashid has nine brothers and sisters. "I guess I spend most of my free time with my family. I really dig them.

"My grandparents are from Morocco—and my family still considers itself Muslim. We go to a Mosque to pray. All our names are Arabic, and sound pretty weird, I guess. There's Hassan and

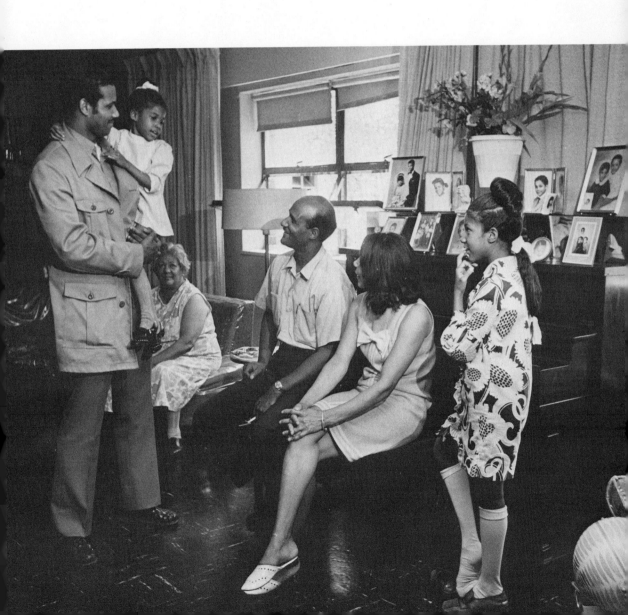

Haroon, Said and Aliah and so on. My wife is pregnant, and our baby will have an Arabic name, too."

Two of Rashid's uncles are policemen, and ever since he was a small boy he wanted to be a policeman. "I thought it was exciting. My father is proud of having a son on the force. At first, my mother didn't want me to join because she thought it was too dangerous. But now she thinks it's beautiful. And that's good because two of my brothers are studying for the police exam.

"My wife didn't want me to be a policeman either. But I think she's gotten used to the idea. She knows it makes me happy."

That night, while Rashid relaxes with his wife, Roy reads a bedtime story to his children. Soon both Roy and Rashid will be asleep. Tomorrow, once again, they will ride the city streets together, knowing that anything could happen that day.

About the Author

RONA BEAME is a free-lance photographer-writer. She has worked for newspapers and magazines, and spent several years as a magazine picture editor. CALLING CAR 24 FRANK: A Day With The Police is her first children's book.

She is a graduate of the University of Michigan, and studied painting at Cooper Union. The mother of three small children, she lives with her husband, a film producer, in New York City.

Books by Rona Beame

CALLING CAR 24 FRANK
A Day with the Police

LADDER COMPANY 108